SATB

MW00760655

Amazing
LOVE!

Recalling Christ's Sacrifice

by Lloyd Larson and Joel Raney

Orchestration by Ed Hogan

Editor: Lloyd Larson
Music Engraving: Linda Taylor
Cover Design: Jeff Richards

© 2016 Lorenz Publishing Company, a division of The Lorenz Corporation.
All rights reserved. Printed in the U.S.A. Reproduction of this publication without permission of
the publisher is a criminal offense subject to prosecution.

Lorenz

A Lorenz Company • www.lorenz.com

Foreword

For several years I served on staff at a church that had a long-standing relationship with the late D. Elton Trueblood, esteemed Quaker theologian and author. One of his profound quotes graced the walls of that church building: *Jesus Christ can be accepted or rejected. He cannot be reasonably ignored.* The teachings of Christ as He ministered among His own people generated the very response of which Trueblood spoke: they either accepted or rejected His claims. There seemed to be no middle ground.

The life and ministry of Jesus is characterized by His extraordinary love for others. For three years He taught, healed, served, and preached the Good News. And yet as He approached the end of those three years, there was a stark contrast between those who embraced His message and those who were skeptical. *Amazing Love!* walks us down the road to the cross as we recount the final hours of our Lord's life when He was rejected, mocked, beaten, and ultimately crucified by the very people He had come to redeem.

Jesus' own words served as a foretelling of what was to come: *Greater love has no one than this, that one lay down his life for his friends. (John 15:13)* The love of God cannot be measured for it has no end. *This is love: not that we loved God, but that He loved us and sent His Son as an atoning sacrifice for our sins. (I John 4:9-10)* That is an amazing kind of love! That is the kind of love–the kind of sacrifice–that commands a personal response. The great hymn writer, Isaac Watts, said it best:

> *Were the whole realm of nature mine, that were a present far too small;*
> *love so amazing, so divine, demands my soul, my life, my all!*

May you find hope in the amazing, sacrificial love of Christ! And may it prompt you to fully embrace the claims of Christ, responding with your very best in devotion and service to the One who gave His best for us.

—Lloyd Larson

Contents

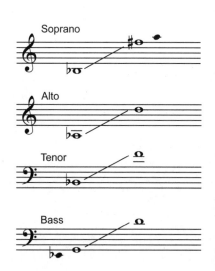

Narration 1

Narrator 1: *(music begins)* The love of God is truly amazing! It has been demonstrated repeatedly from the beginning of time as the Creator has reached out to share unconditional love with you and me.

Narrator 2: This is how God showed His love among us: He sent His one and only Son into the world that we might live through Him. This is love: not that we loved God, but that He loved us and sent His Son as an atoning sacrifice for our sins. *(I John 4:9-10)*

Narrator 1: I have loved you with an everlasting love; I have drawn you with loving-kindness. *(Jeremiah 31:3)*

Some of the cover-art images and graphics from this work are available as free downloads. We hope that you can use them to assist in the making of your bulletins, posters, flyers, website and email announcements, and in any other way that's within your organization and in conjunction with performances of this work.

To access these files, please visit www.lorenz.com/downloads and navigate to the desired folder. PC users should right click and choose "Save Target As…" and Macintosh users should click and hold the link, then choose "Save Target As…" We have provided standard file formats that should be usable in most page layout or word processing software.

Due to the vast number of differences in computer system setups, we are unable to provide technical support for downloadable images/graphics by either phone or email.

Amazing Love!

Words by **Lloyd Larson**
based on **Jeremiah 31:3**
and **Charles Wesley**, 1738

Music by **Lloyd Larson**
Incorporating: MY SAVIOR'S LOVE
by **Charles H. Gabriel**, 1905,
and Quoting SAGINA
by **Thomas Campbell**, 1825

© 2016 Lorenz Publishing Company, a division of The Lorenz Corporation. All rights reserved. Printed in U.S.A.
Reproduction of this publication without permission of the publisher is a criminal offense subject to prosecution.
THE CCLI LICENSE DOES NOT GRANT PERMISSION TO PHOTOCOPY THIS MUSIC.

loved you with an ev - er - last - ing love."

"I have loved you with an ev - er - last - ing love; drawn you with my lov - ing

8

maz - ing love! How can it be that God of all e -

ter - ni - ty should care for me?

mf

A -

maz - ing love! How can it be that God would send His

mf

kind - ness," so says our God who reigns on high; so says our God, cre - a - tor of earth and sky. "I have loved you with an ev - er - last - ing love."_____ A - maz - ing

love! How can it be that Thou, my

How can it be that Thou, my

God,_____ should_____ die? A - maz - ing

God,_____ should_____ die?

love!_____

Narration 2

Narrator 2: The ministry of Jesus was characterized by His extraordinary love for others. For three years He taught, healed, served, and preached the Good News. Now, following the miraculous raising of Lazarus from the dead, Jesus and a joyous crowd of followers prepared to enter Jerusalem in anticipation of the Passover celebration.

Narrator 1: The great crowd that had come for the Feast heard that Jesus was on His way to Jerusalem. They took palm branches and went out to meet Him, shouting "Hosanna! Blessed is He who comes in the name of the Lord! Blessed is the King of Israel!" *(John 12:12-13)*

Lift Up Your Voice and Sing, "Hosanna!"

Words by **Joel Raney** and
Jeannette Threlfall, 1873

Music by **Joel Raney**
Incorporating ELLACOMBE,
Gesangbuch der H. W. K. Hofkapelle, 1784

© 2012 Lorenz Publishing Company, a division of The Lorenz Corporation. All rights reserved. Printed in U.S.A.
Reproduction of this publication without permission of the publisher is a criminal offense subject to prosecution.
THE CCLI LICENSE DOES NOT GRANT PERMISSION TO PHOTOCOPY THIS MUSIC.

comes in the name of the Lord.

Bless-ed is He who

Ho - san - na, ho -

comes in the Lord.

san - na! Bless-ed is He who

comes in the name of the Lord. "Ho-
"Ho-
san - na, ho - san - na!" san - na, in the high - est!" That an - cient song we
That an - cient song we sing, "Ho - san - na, ho-
sing, for Christ is our Re-

18

san - na!"
deem - er, the Lord of heav'n, our King.
The Lord of

heav'n, our King.
O may we ev - er praise Him
with

heart and life and voice,
and in His bliss - ful

presence eternally rejoice, rejoice! Open the gates, Jerusalem.

20

Narration 3

Narrator 1: Even as shouts of "Hosanna!" still echoed in the air, seeds of doubt were being sown by His critics as they openly questioned the claims of Christ. Amid the contrasting scenes of jubilation and skepticism, Jesus arranged to meet with His closest followers to observe the Passover Feast, challenging them to be servants in a world of need as they remembered Him in the days to come.

Narrator 2: Jesus said, "I have eagerly desired to eat this Passover with you before I suffer. For I tell you, I will not eat it again until it finds fulfillment in the kingdom of God." After taking the cup, He gave thanks and said, "Take this and divide it among you. For I tell you I will not drink again of the fruit of the vine until the kingdom of God comes." *(music begins)* And He took bread, gave thanks and broke it, and gave it to them, saying, "This is my body given for you; do this in remembrance of me." *(Luke 22:15-19)*

As You Serve, Remember Me

Words and Music by
Joel Raney

© 2016 Lorenz Publishing Company, a division of The Lorenz Corporation. All rights reserved. Printed in U.S.A.
Reproduction of this publication without permission of the publisher is a criminal offense subject to prosecution.
THE CCLI LICENSE DOES NOT GRANT PERMISSION TO PHOTOCOPY THIS MUSIC.

serve, and as you serve, re-mem-ber Me.

— Go and sat-is-fy the hun-gry, go and

share the bread of life; go and serve, and as you

SA

TB

serve, re-mem-ber Me.

At the

28

end of the jour - ney, at the close of the

day, as the night falls slow - ly, as you

bow your heads to pray, do not let your hearts be

trou-bled, have faith and trust in me, and wher-ev-er I am you will al - so be. At the end of the jour-ney, at the close of the

day, as the night falls slow-ly, as you bow your heads to pray, do not let your hearts be trou-bled, have faith and trust in me, and wher-ev-er I am

pit

Narration 4

Narrator 2: In these intimate moments and the sharing of the Passover meal, Jesus spoke in sobering tones of what was to come. He spoke of these, His faithful followers, who would soon fall away. He spoke of rejection and death, even amid the claims of His disciples that they would never abandon Him.

Narrator 1: Then Jesus went with His disciples to a place called Gethsemane, and He said to them, "Sit here while I go over there and pray." He took Peter and the two sons of Zebedee along with Him, and He began to be sorrowful and troubled. Then He said to them, "My soul is overwhelmed with sorrow to the point of death. Stay here and keep watch with me."

Narrator 2: Going a little farther, He fell with His face to the ground and prayed, "My Father, if it is possible, may this cup be taken from me. Yet not as I will, but as You will." *(Matthew 26:36-39)*

slowd

Alone in the Garden He Prays

Words by **Lloyd Larson** based on
Matthew 26:36, 39 and **Luke 22:44**
and Appalachian Folk Hymn

Music by **Lloyd Larson**
Incorporating WONDROUS LOVE
from *Southern Harmony*, 1835

© 2016 Lorenz Publishing Company, a division of The Lorenz Corporation. All rights reserved. Printed in U.S.A.
Reproduction of this publication without permission of the publisher is a criminal offense subject to prosecution.
THE CCLI LICENSE DOES NOT GRANT PERMISSION TO PHOTOCOPY THIS MUSIC.

www.lorenz.com

won-drous love is this, O my soul!

What won-drous love is this that

caused the Lord of bliss to bear the dread-ful

Narration 5

Narrator 1: The solitude of this garden of prayer was suddenly shattered by the chaos of a large crowd, led by Judas, who had come to arrest Jesus. They took Him to Caiaphas, the High Priest, who was surrounded by teachers of the Law and elders. Numerous false accusations were made during a mock trial, ultimately leading to the decision to hand Jesus over to Pilate, the Roman governor for the region.

Narrator 2: Pilate wanted no part of this lynching, saying that he found no basis for the charges. He repeatedly asked Jesus about His claims and the charges being brought against Him. Ultimately, though, Pilate relented and handed Jesus over to be crucified.

Narrator 1: So the soldiers took charge of Jesus. Carrying His own cross, He went out to the place of the Skull (also called Golgotha). Here they crucified Him, and with Him two others – one on each side and Jesus in the middle. *(John 19:16b-18)*

Behold the Lamb of God!

Words by **Joel Raney** and
attr. **Bernard of Clairvaux**, 12th c.;
tr. **James W. Alexander**, 1830

Music by **Joel Raney**
Incorporating *PASSION CHORALE*
by **Hans Leo Hassler**, 1601

© 2016 Lorenz Publishing Company, a division of The Lorenz Corporation. All rights reserved. Printed in U.S.A.
Reproduction of this publication without permission of the publisher is a criminal offense subject to prosecution.
THE CCLI LICENSE DOES NOT GRANT PERMISSION TO PHOTOCOPY THIS MUSIC.

with nail-scarred hands and a spear for His side,

the Son of Man pre-pares to die. With a loud and

lone - ly cry, un-der-neath a dark - ened sky,

nailed to a cross of wood and hang - ing there to die; as the scorn - ers mock His name, cry-ing out His Fa - ther's name, God's on - ly Son is slain!

Be-hold the Lamb of God!

O sa-cred Head, now wound - ed,____

— with grief and shame____ weighed down,_____ now

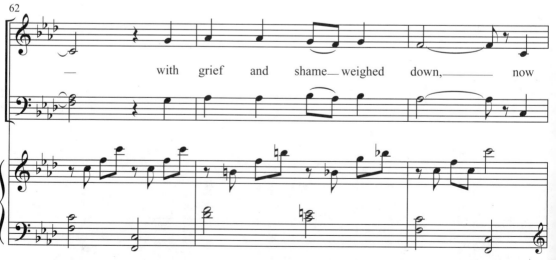

scorn - ful - ly sur - round - ed_____ with thorns, Thine on - ly crown;_____ O sa - cred Head, what glo - ry, what bliss till now was Thine; yet, though de - spised and

go - ry,——— I joy to call Thee mine.

With a loud and lone - ly cry, un-der-neath a dark - ened sky, nailed to a

Tempo I ♩ = ca. 100

The cross of wood and hang-ing there to die; as the scorn-ers mock His name, cry-ing out His Fa-ther's name, God's on-ly Son is slain! Be-hold the Lamb of

Narration 6

Narrator 2: Nailed to a cross to die a criminal's death, Jesus, the living expression of God's incomparable love, took upon Himself the hate and sin of the world. Rejected, mocked, beaten, and now crucified on a tree of guilt, this sinless servant endured a final round of insults from those He had come to save.

Narrator 1: It was now the sixth hour, and darkness came over the whole land until the ninth hour, for the sun stopped shining. And the curtain of the temple was torn in two. Jesus called out with a loud voice, "Father, into your hands I commit my spirit." When He had said this, He breathed His last. The centurion, seeing what had happened, praised God and said, "Surely this was a righteous man." *(Luke 23:44-47)*

How Can It Be?

Words by
Charles Wesley, alt.

Arranged by **Lloyd Larson**
Music: **Pavane, Op. 50**
by **Gabriel Fauré**

© 2012, this arrangement © 2016 Lorenz Publishing Company, a division of The Lorenz Corporation.
All rights reserved. Printed in U.S.A.
Reproduction of this publication without permission of the publisher is a criminal offense subject to prosecution.
THE CCLI LICENSE DOES NOT GRANT PERMISSION TO PHOTOCOPY THIS MUSIC.

60

55/1180&81L-60

62

55/1180&81L-62

64

Narration 7

Narrator 2: A man named Joseph from the town of Arimathea, a member of the Jewish Council who had not supported the decision to crucify Jesus, went to Pilate seeking permission to take Jesus' body to prepare and bury it in a tomb he owned. Pilate granted his request.

Narrator 1: Pilate also granted a request from the chief priests and the Pharisees that the tomb be made secure until the third day so that the disciples could not come and steal the body claiming that Jesus had been raised from the dead.

Narrator 2: After the Sabbath, at dawn on the first day of the week, Mary Magdalene and the other Mary went to look at the tomb. There was a violent earthquake, for an angel of the Lord came down from heaven and, going to the tomb, rolled back the stone and sat on it. His appearance was like lightning, and his clothes were white as snow. The guards were so afraid of him that they shook and became like dead men. The angel said to the women, "Do not be afraid, for I know that you are looking for Jesus who was crucified. He is not here. He has risen, just as He said!" *(Matthew 28:1-6a)*

Christ Is Risen, Sing Alleluia!

Words by **Joel Raney**,
William C. Dix, 1866,
and **Matthew Bridges**, 1851

Music by **Joel Raney**
Incorporating: HYFRYDOL
by **Rowland H. Prichard**, 1830,
and DIADEMATA
by **George J. Elvey**, 1868

Christ is ris - en, sing al - le - lu - ia! lift your voic - es in

© 2016 Lorenz Publishing Company, a division of The Lorenz Corporation. All rights reserved. Printed in U.S.A.
Reproduction of this publication without permission of the publisher is a criminal offense subject to prosecution.
THE CCLI LICENSE DOES NOT GRANT PERMISSION TO PHOTOCOPY THIS MUSIC.

55/1180&81L-69

74

55/1180&81L-74

Death is de - feat - ed, God's plan is com - plet - ed, sing

al - le - lu - ia! Christ is vic - to - ri - ous,

praise Him with glo - ri - ous hymns, mar - vel - ous hymns, glo - ri - ous

Narration 8

Narrator 1: The gracious love of God was demonstrated in the sending of the Messiah – the very Son of God – to live among us. Jesus lived a humble life of love, ultimately sacrificing His life so that we might experience the gift of eternal life. That kind of sacrifice…that kind of amazing love…deserves nothing less than my very best in response. God's gracious gift demands my life, my all!

Narrator 2: Greater love has no one than this, that one lay down his life for his friends. *(John 15:13)*

Narrator 1: Who shall separate us from the love of Christ? Shall trouble or hardship or persecution or famine or nakedness or danger or sword? No, in all these things we are more than conquerors through Him who loved us.

Narrator 2: For I am convinced that neither death nor life, neither angels nor demons, neither the present nor the future, nor any powers, neither height nor depth, nor anything else in all creation, will be able to separate us from the love of God that is in Christ Jesus our Lord. *(Romans 8:35, 37-39)*

Amazing Love Demands My All!

Words by **Lloyd Larson**
based on **Jeremiah 31:3**
and **Isaac Watts**, 1707

Arranged with New Music
by **Lloyd Larson**
Tunes: SAGINA by **Thomas Campbell**, 1825
and HAMBURG by **Lowell Mason**, 1824

© 2016 Lorenz Publishing Company, a division of The Lorenz Corporation. All rights reserved. Printed in U.S.A.
Reproduction of this publication without permission of the publisher is a criminal offense subject to prosecution.
THE CCLI LICENSE DOES NOT GRANT PERMISSION TO PHOTOCOPY THIS MUSIC.

earth and sky. "I have loved you with an

ev - er - last - ing love."

When I sur -

count but loss, and pour con - tempt on

all my pride.

For - bid it, Lord, that I should boast,

save in the death of Christ, my God; all the vain things that charm me most, all the vain things that charm me most, I sac-ri-fice them

far too small;

poco rit.

a tempo ff

love so a - maz - ing, so di -

vine, de - mands my soul, my